29.99

D1326371

Forbidden Places

Exploring our abandoned heritage

Sylvain Margaine

Texts David Margaine

Jonglez

Introduction

Forgotten places. Unlisted ruins.
Dead ends of a consumer society.
Today, it is less expensive to start from scratch than to renovate or restore.

This foray into contemporary ruins is but a brief glimpse of a project started more than ten years ago. At first, the objective was documentary. The aesthetic beauty of abandonment naturally emerged to finally become a primary part of the project.

Industrial wastelands, abandoned castles, deserted churches, hospitals or convents ... So many sites left in neglect following a relocation, bankruptcy, inheritance or an unfortunate event.
Some places played a role in history. Others are the result of Pharaonic projects that were never completed, the fruit of the vagaries of several decades of grandeur that eventually slid into oblivion.

Half of them no longer even exist. For others, time will take its toll, or the bulldozers will.
Only a small number, saved from destruction, shall rise once again after extensive reconstruction.

I wish you a great journey on the other side of the mirror of our industrial societies, in the heart of abandoned worlds.

Sylvain Margaine, June 2009

Contents

For Hector and Sidonie, future explorers...

Beelitz Sanatorium

Potsdam, Germany

Beelitz Sanatorium

Beelitz, care for the soul and the body.

Despite its glacial cold spells, this city tucked away in the heart of the Brandenburg forest has for over a thousand years welcomed all kinds of visitors: pilgrims coming to celebrate the miracle of the Eucharist, Prussian soldiers (and deserters), then the Bundeswehr conscripts garrisoned there. As a place of welcome, it was natural for the city to set up a hospital complex.

What other activity could be better suited to Beelitz?

In 1898, with the construction of sixty buildings, Beelitz Heistatten became one of the largest sanatoriums in the world.

Before there were antibiotics, the fresh air sweeping over this plain must have seemed a guarantee of healthiness and well-being. In addition, everything had been laid out to ensure the residents' tranquility: balconies and terraces for each wing, patios dotted among wooded walks, sports halls, several boiler rooms for optimal temperature control, independent cooking facilities, and more. The hospital even had its own power station, commensurate with the size of the place.

Germany entered into a conflict that would change the destiny of the Western world.

The sanatorium was converted into a military hospital. So it would remain until it closed, in 1995.

Many a person affected by the fighting would come to take a cure of several days or several months in the shelter of its walls. A certain Adolf Hitler, wounded in the thigh at the Battle of the Somme, stayed there between October and November 1916.

After the German defeat and the division of the German territory, the state of Brandenburg was handed over to the East.

The healthcare establishment thus followed its destiny to the advantage of the Red Army, followed by the Soviet Union and its satellite countries.

Modernisation was carried out over the years — lifts, examination rooms, operating theatres — preserving the architecture of Heino Schmieden. The Russian patients would continue to stay there long after the reunification, as it was not until 1995 that they abandoned the hospital.

Beelitz Sanatorium, Potsdam, Germany

The conversion of this vast complex is tricky. After several attempts, only a few wings have been refurbished as a neurological research and rehabilitation centre.

As for the miles of abandoned corridors and the numerous neglected services, they are gradually falling into oblivion in the pine forest south of Berlin.

Beelitz Sanatorium, Potsdam, Germany

Beelitz Sanatorium, Potsdam, Germany

Beelitz Sanatorium, Potsdam, Germany

Veterinary School

They were the stars of the place.

It was an acquired habit.

Feeling yourself watched, observed, spied on.

Dissected.

After several years, they began to get a taste for it!

Constantly rubbing shoulders with students, future vets, and experts in the making inevitably had quite an effect on them.

So their behaviour was exemplary!

When the faculty was relocated, they didn't believe it and stayed to guard one of the site's twenty buildings.

Put out to pasture?

After thirty years of loyal service?

Impossible!

They knew it would happen. The beauty of the neo-Romantic façades could not fail to come under the spotlight once again.

Veterinary School

In 1990, the only researchers were estate agents and the architectural complex was bought up piecemeal for conversion into apartments.

Who will have the courage to evict the last residents, possibly as old as the buildings themselves?

A century old and still just as fresh?

Laboratory animals keep well when they're marinating in formaldehyde …

Veterinary School, Brussels, Belgium

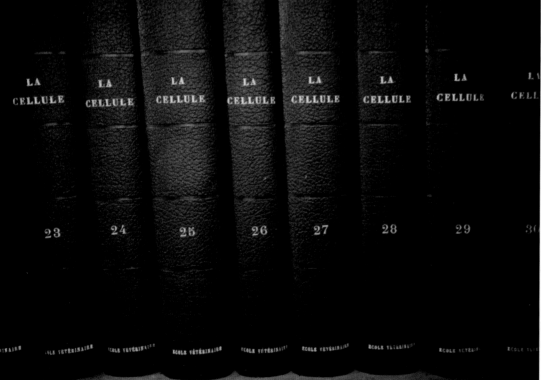

Veterinary School, Brussels, Belgium

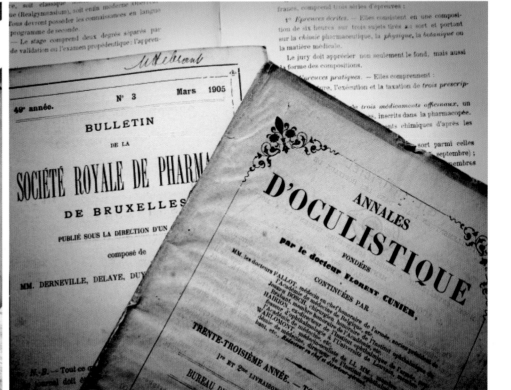

Veterinary School, Brussels, Belgium

Chez Madame La Baronne

Channel Islands

Would you care to take a bath before going into the sitting room?
Take your time and make yourself at home, Madame la Baronne is very patient.

You haven't brought all your toiletries?
Don't worry, you'll find everything you need here.
Of course, the utensils are a little, shall we say, old-fashioned.

But for your convenience everything has been left out for you.
Here, you see, nothing has changed.
So don't be surprised if the furniture is a little faded.

We live in the old style, you know.
On the other hand, if you want to rest, you'll be completely satisfied.

Absolute calm.

The household activity won't disturb you in any way.
There hasn't been much of that for a long time anyway.
If you don't mind dust, you can stretch out in peace and quiet on the beds.
And the sheets
Of another age.

Chez Madame La Baronne, Îles Anglo-Normandes

Chez Madame La Baronne

You'll have noticed that Madame la Baronne is the owner of a vast estate.

Since the death of her husband, this great lady devotedly carries on her mission of hospitality.

For her, nothing has basically changed since the days of salons and receptions.

You'd think that her house was following this noble tradition with the same rigour.

Nothing has moved

Only time has passed.

And settled itself, a perpetual guest, in the dusty corridors of the neglected house.

The only one still here is the Baroness who year after year still watches over her slumbering home.

Would you care to stay for the night?

Chez Madame La Baronne, Channel Islands

Chez Madame La Baronne, Channel Islands

Chez Madame La Baronne, Channel Islands

Antwerp Premetro

The metro is still sleeping,
In a sleep growing lighter.

Down the years the concrete gives it life.

Another gallery is attached.

And the network grows.

In the open air or underground, the engines drag their passengers ever further, ever deeper.

The lines tunnelled over thirty years, and those still to be cut, will eventually meet in the very roots of the city of Antwerp.

Is this an unconscious quest for roots?

The flagrantly urban nature of the work seems like a dive into the very heart of our civilisation.

Antwerp Premetro

It's the earth that is pierced and yet it's the earth that is hidden.

Illuminated, varnished, polished.

As if to be forgotten.

What is there to hide from the hurrying travellers who always rush into the trains at departure time?

Perhaps their human condition, which they themselves have hidden under their city suits.

Too clean, too healthy.

In respect for the tacit protocols accepted and respected by members of the community.

Luckily, there will always be a forerunner, a premetro, bound with scaffolding and poured concrete and a successor, closed lines abandoned and left to themselves

Maybe somebody will find a photograph of the journey to remind us that these projects are only a small scratch, an ephemeral witness to our passage on earth.

Antwerp Premetro, Antwerp, Belgium

Hôpital de la Marine

Rochefort, Charente-Maritime, France

A calling.

The habitual daily routine has never concerned them.
They preferred the Nation,
or their ambitions,
to a life spent stagnating in the same house.

They chose to join up and sail off to fight.

At least against the winds and the tides.

Wishing to lighten the burden of those who had done their duty by it, the homeland has offered very high quality healthcare facilities since the seventeenth century.

Soldiers and sailors returning from exotic expeditions, as well as the artisans building the ships, were treated at the maritime hospital of Rochefort, with patient care that was described as second to none at the time.

Not only were the staff efficient, but the patients' convalescence was brightened as everything was planned to ease their days of pain.

Hôpital de la Marine

The architectural aesthetic, in a bungalow style, let in the sunlight. For the well-being of the patients. For those who no longer had any hope of recovery, the buildings included a parish church and two chapels.

The fact that this establishment was home to the first school of military medicine in Europe, and the oldest school of naval medicine in the world, bears out its importance.

Just like the patients, the future doctors were well looked after: accommodation was provided, but they could also study in a library stocking tens of thousands of works, and a vast lecture hall.

The hospice has been modernised over the years without losing its original beauty.
Yet the hospital, no longer meeting modern hygiene standards, closed in 1983.

The building, with its solid foundations, found a purchaser who divided it into apartments.

Unlisted, part of the complex has still to be taken over.

Let's hope that a good buyer will come to the rescue before it's too late.

Hôpital de la Marine, Rochefort, Charente Maritime, France

Hôpital de la Marine, Rochefort, Charente Maritime, France

Hôpital de la Marine, Rochefort, Charente Maritime, France

Cane Hill Asylum

Its wide corridors spread out in space and time.
For 120 years, Cane Hill contained the insanity of its residents.

Up to 2,000 patients at a time.
Following its creation in 1882, it saw the treatment of its patients evolve.
From a collective mental home to solitary cells.
From cold showers to chemical straitjackets.
From pious gatherings to art therapy.
This hospital saw it all and was recognised.
As first rate.

The names of eminent patients were noted in the registers:
Faithful to the house maxim, Mrs Chaplin, mother, Mr Bowie, brother, thus came here to soothe their troubled minds.
Difficult to always be trendy ...
The size of the site and its large number of buildings finally became overwhelming.
One by one the patients left for more modern establishments.
The centre closed its doors in the 1990s.

For a decade, it was abandoned.
During this period, it had to cope with flood and fire.
Was it just badly located, or was it bad luck?
Attempts at reclassification or conversion have failed repeatedly.
There's no future for this piece of English history.
In the end the wrecking ball will get the better of Cane Hill.

Cane Hill Asylum, Coulsdon, London Borough of Croydon, England

Cane Hill Asylum, Coulsdon, London Borough of Croydon, England

Cane Hill Asylum, Coulsdon, London Borough of Croydon, England

Château Bijou

Just like the big boys!

Originally a gentleman's residence in 1763, over the years this building has been decked out with everything a castle could desire: frescoes, marble pillars and a neo-Gothic chapel with stained-glass windows. These embellishments, carried out in the twentieth century, rather detract from its authenticity …

Snug in the heart of the Béarnaise countryside, bordered by a lake and an extremely pleasant park with numerous fountains, Château Bijou was used as a holiday home by its last owner, Madame Combes.

On her death, the estate continued to be maintained, before being taken over by a Friendly Society. Police officers on leave could then enjoy the privilege of this architectural gem until the 1990s. Abandoned, Château Bijou was in turn vandalised, looted, and suffered a fire.

The local residents, not wanting to see this highly unusual structure fall into ruin, succeeded in having the entire property listed as a historic monument in 2008.

Since then, several projects have been drawn up for the petit palais.

Perseverance is sometimes rewarded.

Château Bijou, Labastide-Villefranche, Pyrénées-Atlantiques, France

Château Bijou, Labastide-Villefranche, Pyrénées-Atlantiques, France

Château Bijou, Labastide-Villefranche, Pyrénées-Atlantiques, France

Château Bijou, Labastide-Villefranche, Pyrénées-Atlantiques, France

La Chartreuse Fort

Soldiers of the 123rd Transport Regiment, your Liège barracks are under attack.

Take up battle positions.
Remember.

1870.
Intended to protect the Dutch forces, it had only ever been used as a barracks,
but it was *your* barracks.

Affirmative.

The French tore it from you in 1914.
You took it back again.

Lost it again in the next conflict,
The Allies snatched it from the Germans in 1944.

In accordance with their sense of honour, the French allowed their comrades to install their "28th General Hospital US Army" there for a while.

Then they laid down their kitbags there once again.

Weren't they well-off there?

La Chartreuse Fort, Liège, Belgium

The remains of German dungeons undermined the morale of the new recruits, but was that any reason to decamp?

Negative.

They served the nation and knew how to live.
The proof is in the frescoes left by the squaddies of the time.

So deserting the barracks and letting them rot, that doesn't appeal to me at all.

There's a time for everything.

What I see is that this cursed time is running out.

As for the fort, it's falling apart.

La Chartreuse Fort, Liège, Belgium

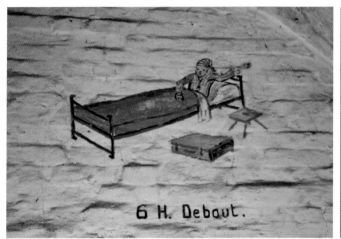

6 H. Debout.

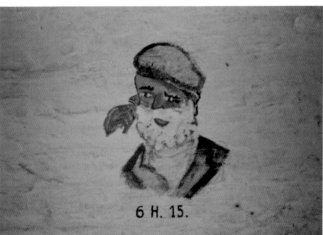

6 H. 15.

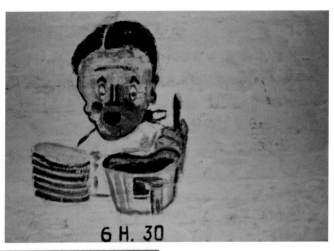

6 H. 30

7 H. 45

10 H.

22 H. Au Lit.

La Chartreuse Fort, Liège, Belgium

La Chartreuse Fort, Liège, Belgium

La Chartreuse Fort, Liège, Belgium

Canfranc Station

"The Pyrenees no longer exist!"

Would the mountains have taken their revenge on such pretentiousness, reaffirming their unmoving superiority in the face of human restlessness?

This invective launched in 1928 by Alfonso XIII, king of Spain, at the inauguration of the international station of Canfranc didn't bring him much luck.

It took some twenty years of labour, as many international treaties, and technical advances never before attempted, in order to link two countries through this station, the largest in Europe.

The challenge thrown at the mountains seemed to have been won!

But despite its three floors, all marble and stone ripped out of the mountains themselves, glass, steel and reinforced concrete, the structure cannot boast of having attained the objectives set by its builders.

From the outset, the wooden ticket offices did not attract the expected crowds. The atmosphere of international crisis that enveloped the Western world in the 1930s probably played a part in this.

As the years went by, tensions grew.

1936, war broke out in Spain.

Traffic was interrupted, the tunnels walled up.

Canfranc Station, Canfranc, Aragon, Spain

The railway came back into service with the surrender of the Republican army and became quite important, this time in the service of the occupying Germans: gold for tungsten. Some 90 tons of ingots in payment for this ore, indispensable for arms production, were transported via Canfranc.

In return, the wagons were also used to move around resistance workers, refugees and Allied forces.

Alas, once the armistice was signed, General Franco, fearing infiltration, closed the line.

– Second interruption –

It was nevertheless reopened in 1948.

With Europe at peace and reconstruction beginning, it might be thought that Canfranc and its station would at last be able to work at full capacity. The site included several restaurants, a vast luxury hotel, offices and even an infirmary just waiting to be used. Unfortunately, all was not smooth going. The line was mainly used by local people unhappy with the long wait and the formalities involved in crossing the border. Passengers and luggage had to change trains at every stop, because the gauge of the tracks was incompatible!

The line was unprofitable.

The infrastructure was poorly maintained, and side tracks feeding the line were even lifted and sent for use in funicular railways in the Alps.

Canfranc was not the hub it was supposed to be.

Friday 27 March 1970. The Aspe valley was buried in snow. The rails were covered in ice. Because of the severe weather and the poor state of the track, freight train 4227 leaving that morning from Pau began to lose its grip, then slid back down the steep slope that it had been attempting to climb. It finished its trajectory in the waters of Gave d'Aspe after demolishing the metal bridge at l'Estanguet.

Miraculously, there were no casualties.

As for the line, it would never recover.

By a combination of shortsighted planning and technical problems, the bridge was never repaired. No more trains would cross the Pyrenees as far as Canfranc.

Open to all comers, the immense building quickly fell into disrepair. On sections of rail a few orphaned wagons still wait for an improbable departure under the eternal gaze of the snowy peaks.

The station itself is ruined.

Terminus?

That would have ignored its beauty: the mixture of classicism and Art Nouveau in the French style, the impressive proportions – seventy-five doors on each side, "more windows than there are days in the year" – the magnificence of the central hall seduced developers.

In early 2006, the bulldozers moved in to begin restoration work.

If all goes well, a complex including a high-class hotel, skating rink, and casino, will be created.

So the station is saved.

As for the line, its fate still lies in the hands of future speculators …

Canfranc Station, Canfranc, Aragon, Spain

Canfranc Station, Canfranc, Aragon, Spain

Hudson River Hospital

State of New York, United States

Thirty years.
Working like crazy to build the Hudson River State Hospital according to the plans of Dr Kirkbride.
The exorbitant construction costs meant that it would be impossible to fully respect the canons of this therapeutic architecture.

The grandeur and majesty intended to contribute to the patients' treatment were nevertheless achieved in the generous proportions of the neo-Gothic buildings:
two wings, initially planned as symmetrical, face each other.
Each was intended to house 300 patients.
One was for men.
The other, for women, ended up smaller.
Separating them, a chapel.

The risk of promiscuity that could raise the patients' temperatures was thus avoided.
Beside the sacred building, the administrative block.
All around, greenery.

Pavilions built to house patients, some of them with serious disorders, were scattered around the park.
The layout was planned so as to make things restful for the residents.

In 1871, the year the complex opened, forty patients were admitted.
Eighty years later, 6,000 were being treated at Hudson River.

The construction costs ruined the developers, and the operating costs were just as high.
The cost of heating, water treatment, distribution and maintenance were equivalent to that of a respectable town.

With the introduction of a new approach to psychiatry, patients were less routinely hospitalised. The administration took advantage of this by closing some services. One after another they were abandoned with the gradual departure of the inmates.

At the end of the 1970s, the two main wings were closed.
Decay became inevitable.
Yet nothing was destroyed.
In the 1990s, a more modern and rational psychiatric institution opened nearby.

Ten years later, Hudson closed its doors.

Vast and still imposing, the building was sold to be renovated into apartments and a commercial centre.

In 2007, when a fire damaged one of the wings, already dilapidated by years of neglect, no restoration work was undertaken.

Awaiting an uncertain future, the site is used as a shooting range for police training.

Law and Order reign at last.

Hudson River Hospital, State of New York, United States

Hudson River Hospital, State of New York, United States

Hudson River Hospital, State of New York, United States

Hudson River Hospital, State of New York, United States

Maastricht Casemates

Maastricht, the Netherlands

Maastricht,
The cradle of history.
A bridge of departure at the crossroads.
Site of numerous epics.
The town has long been obliged to protect itself.
The Dutch Republic, the Spanish, the French ...
So much hostility turned Maastricht into a fortified place with numerous ramparts.
The first walls date from the Roman Empire. Over the centuries and successive conflicts, the fortifications were modernised and helped the city resist the assaults of its attackers.

A major element of the military strategy was mastery of the underground spaces. This allowed plans to be developed for defence, observation, approach, and even preparation for attack. A number of galleries formed an elaborate underground network.
An alternative circuit.
Favourable to the most cunning of strategies.

The quality of the construction of the corridors, in brick and shale, bears witness to the importance of these passages.
A lot of time was spent here.
A lot of people met here.
There are still inscriptions,
a date, a name ...
W. Hofman, 1724, hastily engraved at the foot of a vault over a crossing.

Maastricht Casemates

Miles of passages, drainage systems, booby traps, with light mines and ammunition rooms.
Here and there one came across casemates, temporary shelters for exhausted soldiers and the nerve centres of these underground galleries.
Military tactics change.

Having nothing to protect but themselves, these shelters were dismantled in 1868.
But the hour of glory of the Maastricht tunnels was not over. From 1941 to 1944, they were equipped with bunkers that could hold over 30,000 civilians fleeing from air raids. The rest of the network continued to be used as a hideout by the Allies.

Today, in peacetime, the guides who have replaced the infantry walk the hushed visitors through the corridors open to the public.

Only one section is accessible to barges.

A warning for wanderers. Many underground defensive systems have been dispersed throughout the dark maze of obscure passages: concealed powder magazines, routes blocked off by one-way doors …

The underground galleries of Maastricht don't seem ready to surrender to the attacking forces yet.

Maastricht Casemates, Maastricht, the Netherlands

Maastricht Casemates, Maastricht, the Netherlands

Maastricht Casemates, Maastricht, the Netherlands

La Villa Sainte Marie

It seems …

At least,
the rumour spreads.

By word of mouth.
As far as the neighbour
Who will only tell her nearest and dearest
Still in whispers.

In any case, the result can be felt:
The place is well and truly empty.

And contains an undeniably staunchly guarded secret.
Too much?

How can one not be overcome by the heaviness of the atmosphere?
In each room there floats an excess of emotion.

Unreasonable.

How can the secret of this home, which has itself stepped back in time, be revealed?

Villa Sainte Marie, Grand Duchy of Luxembourg

La Villa Sainte Marie

Yet everything seems to be in place.
The bed made,
the knick-knacks arranged,
the bottles sorted.

All seems in order
Put away?
Shut away?

The omnipresent Christ-like gaze will not leave the conscience alone.

Each room transcends our perception of faith.

For a snapshot in time, we try not to be overawed.

The visit over, we leave Sainte Marie relieved,
Almost as if pushed outside.

Leaving this abode to its muted silence, we leave without revealing what really happened here.

A misfortune? A confidence?

Would it be wise to be in on the secret?

God alone knows …

Villa Sainte Marie, Grand Duchy of Luxembourg

Villa Sainte Marie, Grand Duchy of Luxembourg

Villa Sainte Marie, Grand Duchy of Luxembourg

Villa Sainte Marie, Grand Duchy of Luxembourg

Villa Sainte Marie, Grand Duchy of Luxembourg

Clabecq Steelworks

Tubize, Walloon Brabant, Belgium

It's as if the earth was dying.
For lack of a meal.
Run out of steel, out of money.

The machine is derailed,
The region has failed.

After having glowed for 350 years, and spread out its steel
arms over 80 hectares, the forge is breathless.
Clabecq is surrendering its soul.

Yet the Brabant territory did all it could for the health of
its machinery.
The engine ran dry?

On the orders of Napoleon I, the flow was diverted until
it lapped at his feet.

At the time they were thought to be of bronze.
For a steelworks, who would have thought that they were
actually of clay?

The innards had to be fed, the conduits gorged with raw
materials and energy.
The vital organs sated themselves on wind, coal, steam,
and the sweat of men.
All in thrall to its development.

Clabecq Steelworks, Tubize, Walloon Brabant, Belgium

Clabecq Steelworks

1850, the "Fonderie et platinerie de fer" of Edouard Goffin was booming.
The blast furnaces rose up even more.
A little more.

Steel was turned into silver.

It was sold far beyond the borders.

The reddened metal, burning material fused in the rolling mills ran over the entire earth.
Ships, railways …

Easy to live, when there is a demand to satisfy.

But,
A century passed.
Times changed.

It was no longer goods that were exported
but the labour force that was outsourced.

The machines were sold off like common scrap.
The forges had no spirit left.

Workers against bankers.
Is progress necessary?

Clabecq Steelworks, Tubize, Walloon Brabant, Belgium

1993, the country stirred itself to save this plant, but the years of struggle served no purpose: three years later, it went bankrupt.
After the state classed it as a disused industrial site, the plant was condemned to imminent destruction.

Last undertaking: abandonment.
As if oblivion was necessary.
Clabecq will not forge the memories of future generations.

Clabecq Steelworks, Tubize, Walloon Brabant, Belgium

Clabecq Steelworks, Tubize, Walloon Brabant, Belgium

Clabecq Steelworks, Tubize, Walloon Brabant, Belgium

Clabecq Steelworks, Tubize, Walloon Brabant, Belgium

Clabecq Steelworks, Tubize, Walloon Brabant, Belgium

Lorette Convent

My very dear sisters,
Have no fear.
We have chosen to follow the orders of Notre Dame de Lorette, let us keep faith in her word.

The miracle she relates of the transportation of the house of Nazareth should reassure us: the story of the band of angels raising up Mary's home to save it from the clutches of the Saracens is echoed in this place.

After more than a century of service to others and education, our convent has closed.

Have the doors that we shut behind us been stolen?
We were just being tested, they have been found again.

There is a reason why our building has been preserved since 1850.

Even though the wishes of the Almighty must be expressed through the purse of a developer or the plans of an architect.

Believe me, our convent may be in decline but it will not perish.

Lorette Convent, Nord, France

Lorette Convent, Nord, France

Newark County Jail

For having held people captive on pretext of their guilt.

For having kept under lock and key a growing number of individuals in degrading conditions.

For having crammed over 2,500 detainees into three floors, cramming them in with complete disregard for privacy or humanity.

For having piled up stone and steel with the sole aim of containing the jailbirds even more.

For having exercised this right since 1837 with no real opportunity of reform for the inmates.

For having by its laxness perpetuated and reproduced what was going on in the outside world:
– Violent and bigoted relationships
– Trafficking of psychotropic substances
– A clannish hierarchy among the Afrikan National Ujaama, Crips, Trinitarios, Latin Kings, Five Percenters and other New Jersey gangs
– Minimal access to cultural activities

For having organised homicides in the name of implementing justice, by various means under different styles of sentencing.

Finally, for having continued after 1970, once all official use was over, to give shelter to traffickers and drug users in a totally illegal "squat",

The penal institution of Newark should be condemned to be left to its own devices and to lapse into a rapid but well-deserved decrepitude.

So be it.

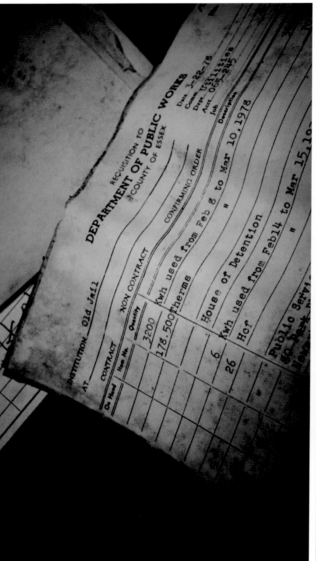

Locomotive Graveyard

Belgium

A silent engine rests on its axles.
The network of tracks seems to have left it behind among the grass growing around and over its edges.
If we go past it and follow the track, we notice other motorised monsters further along.

Buffalo, Edelweiss, Pacific,
All transfixed in a steely sleep.
Arranged in serried ranks in ice-cold hangars, they wait in vain to be revved up again.

Hertz is no longer on the itinerary.
Left alone against a buffer at the end of the platform, some rust away for not being able to operate their pistons.
Opposite lie the sleeping-cars with their illusive luxury.
No matter their class.
Henceforth it is difficult to control the draughts, those ultimate and elusive visitors.

They whistle for a split second below the windows of the lounge car then slip unpretentiously away over the ballast, indifferent to its temptations.

Near the exit, a last locomotive, the guard's van, sadly contemplates a sleeper that it will never cross again.

There is no longer any room for doubt.
We have discovered the cemetery of the railway species.

Locomotive Graveyard, Belgium

Locomotive Graveyard, Belgium

Locomotive Graveyard, Belgium

Fort Portalet

The small gateway.

Carved out of the flanks of the Pyrenees outlining the Somport Pass, it reflects the ambivalence of the links that can be woven between transborder counterparts.
We will never know who really started it ...

The stronghold of Poutou, medieval ancestor of Fort Portalet, was originally conceived as a tollbooth in response to the one installed by the Iberian neighbours a few kilometres away.

This role lasted until 1789, when the fort mutated into a military post, a valuable asset that protected the pass leading to the French Pyrenees during the Spanish wars of the next century.

1842, Louis Philippe ordered the construction of a new fort a few hundred metres away.

The craggy peaks slowed the building work without however stopping it. 2,200 m^2 of buildings, 700 m^2 of tunnels cut directly into the mountainside.

In an attempt at impregnability, the construction was only linked to the route it overlooked by a single access: the Pont d'Enfer. This stone footbridge with two central arches spanned the Aspe mountain stream that hurtled down several hundred metres below.

The 18th infantry regiment of the town of Pau was given the responsibility of occupying the fort.

Fort Portalet

The valley was enclosed,
The fort blending in with its landscape.

Its different sections – the guardroom, the barracks, the officers' mess and the powder magazine – were spread out on various levels.

Blending into the scenery, Le Portalet thus acquired its very characteristics, dark and damp.

Despite the beauty of the landscape opening out before them, the occupants were scarcely envied by their occasional visitors. Some even felt sorry for the fort's defenders, with the sepulchral atmosphere of the compound making itself so heavily felt.

The most surprising fact is that, forsaken by the army in 1925, the place was used for a decade as a holiday camp for the 80 Cadets of Notre-Dame de Bordeaux.

With the 1939–1945 hostilities, the fort rediscovered its military uses and became a political prison for the Axis forces. Many prisoners were incarcerated there, including Blum, Daladier, Gamelin, Mandel and Reynaud.

After their liberation by members of the resistance from the Aspe valley, it was the turn of the losers to go and serve their time in the bleak cells. Pétain was locked up there for six months, during which he had all the time in the world to meditate on the conditions of incarceration of his former enemies.

As Franco-Spanish relations eased, Europe found peace again. In 1962, the army decided to part with this burdensome ally, decommissioned by the War Ministry. It put the fort up for sale.

Due to its poor reputation, or austere features, hoteliers' rehabilitation projects failed.
Mother Nature found herself the sole occupant of the building that was falling into ruin.

Thirty years would pass before the authorities realised the importance of preserving the edifice, at last listed as a historic monument.

The story thus began again in 2004 with the first clean-up project.

The fort was brought up to date.

No longer a matter of defence or imprisonment, Portalet will throw open its gates to tourists thirsting for history ... and black dungeons.

Fort Portalet, Col du Somport, Pyrénées-Atlantiques, France

Fort Portalet, Col du Somport, Pyrénées-Atlantiques, France

Fort Portalet, Col du Somport, Pyrénées-Atlantiques, France

Val Saint-Lambert Crystal Glassworks

Serve us a goblet then,
but not just any one,
a Val Saint-Lambert if you please.

Of glass, of crystal,
But local.
The real thing.

Believe me, since 1825, they've seen everything.
Wood, coal, steam
And above all much sweat.
No doubt about it, masses have come together here.
Glad to be taken on: lodgings, school, savings accounts
for sickness or for retirement.
They knew how to care for the workforce.
And the workforce, for its part, was master of the trade.
Luxury, high quality.
And the products can be seen in fine houses all over the
world.

What about the wars?
No worries, when the craftsmanship is good.
There's no reason why the business should fail.

Unless …

Over the years, they automated, they progressed.
The factory was linked to the railway system; it had an
independent gas and electricity supply. Even the kilns
were made on the spot.

Val Saint-Lambert Crystal Glassworks, Seraing, Liège region, Belgium

Yet the times were not propitious for luxury goods.
So they tried to streamline production before handing it over to the speculators.
Nothing came of that; the glassmakers' boom was shattered.
In August 2008, the Val Saint-Lambert Glassworks Company was declared bankrupt.
The end of a 182-year-old history?

Apparently not, because after three months of negotiations the company was bought out.
Work can start again.

So let's drink to its health!

Val Saint-Lambert Crystal Glassworks, Seraing, Liège region, Belgium

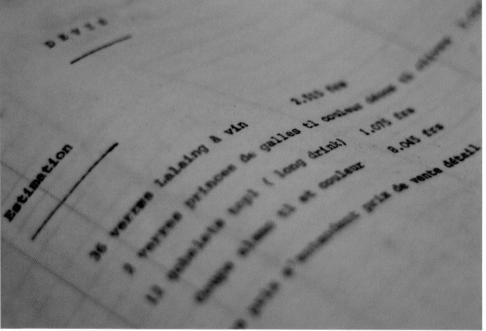

Val Saint-Lambert Crystal Glassworks, Seraing, Liège region, Belgium

Kent School

Hostert.

A place of contemplation.

During the 500 years of these stone walls' existence, many communities have come and gone.

Generous donations meant that the Franciscan monks could add a church and school at the beginning of the 20th century. In this way they founded a hospice for invalids and the mentally ill. The community lived independently and prospered, doing agricultural work. It even acquired some fame through the very popular services of its choir.

The Nazi party, hostile to this religious order, put an end to this state of bliss, overburdening the followers of St Francis with taxes. They were forced to give up part of their property to the province.
It is sadly not difficult to guess the fate of the monks' former patients: the National Socialist party began by sterilising them and then deported them to other centres.

Thus the "special unit for children" was opened, where all young people declared abnormal were sent. Doctor Wesse, assisted by two nurses, was responsible for what happened to the unfortunate ones who fell into their hands.

The service, closed in 1943, was cleared of its occupants, who were sent to finish their short lives in other special units.

Kent School, Hostert, North Rhine-Westphalia, Germany

Kent School

In all, during the conflict, almost 500 children died in this institution and more than 1,000 others passed through before meeting much the same fate.

Meanwhile, throughout the war, the religious community held the title deeds of the property. In 1952, the Franciscan brothers took it over once again. Weakened as they were, they could not carry on their work and rented part of the buildings to the Allies.
Decline threatened already: a new church built nearby put an end to the services at Waldniel Hostert.

The British, settling into their rented accommodation, opened a modern hospital and in 1963 a school, in response to growing demand. As many as 6,000 pupils were enrolled. The student community of Kent School is still lively.

The listed site has not yet found a new role since the gradual retreat of the Allies left it empty.

Even the former cemetery converted in 1988 to a memorial for the victims of the Nazi euthanasia campaign is today turning to wasteland.

As if time's strong desire to move forward has made it forget the past.

Kent School, Hostert, North Rhine-Westphalia, Germany

Kent School, Hostert, North Rhine-Westphalia, Germany

Between death and oblivion
the body must sometimes undergo
tests.
Before being laid to rest.
In the tranquility of legality.
Thanatos comes to the aid of logic.

Thus, at the least suspicion science interferes.
Auxiliary to justice, it slices, weighs and measures.
With its customary sharpness, it calls on steel in the search for truth.
Under the theatre lamps the forensic scientists and their assistants are at work.

Why then did the deceased so quickly fail his alter-ego?
Far from esoteric rites and funereal liturgies, the practitioner carries out his sterile work on a subject that he will not cure.
The lips of his patient remain closed; his approach must be rigorous if he is to make the flesh speak.

The examination must be successful. The candidates passing through flock to the gate to obtain their certificates.

Protected by the graveyard that surrounds it, the Schoonselhof Forensic Institute could also have rested in peace. However, its burial plot has been taken away.

Nobody really has the right to a concession for life.

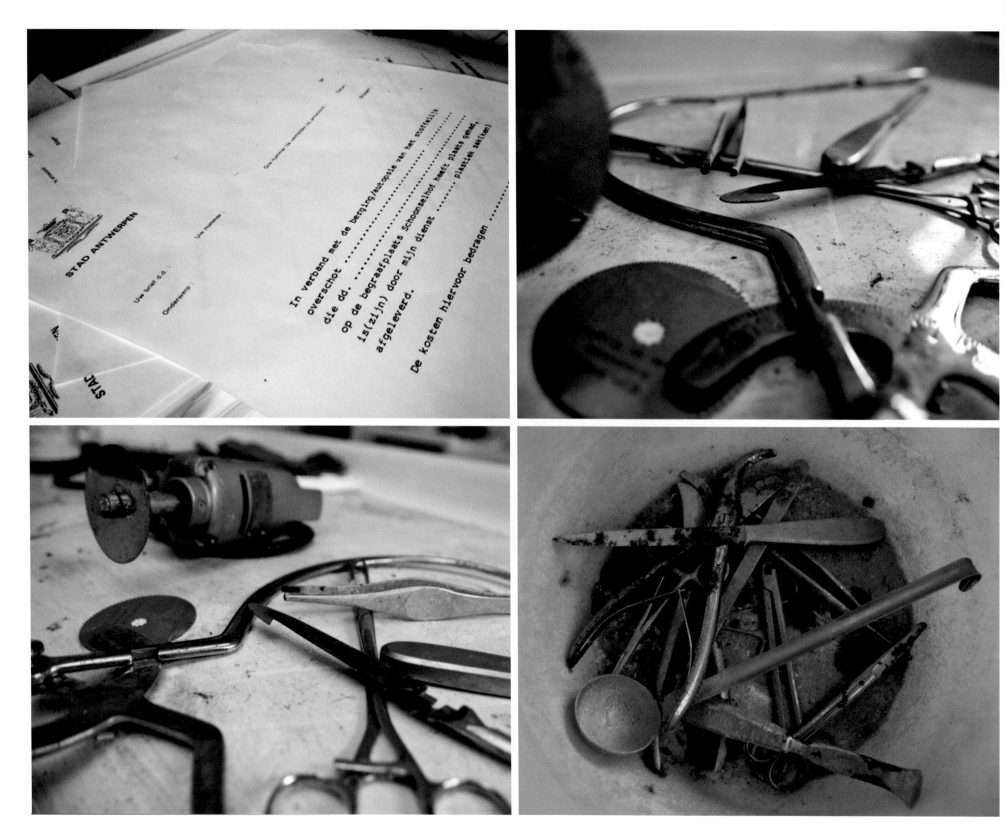

Forensic Institute, Antwerp, Belgium

Forensic Institute, Antwerp, Belgium

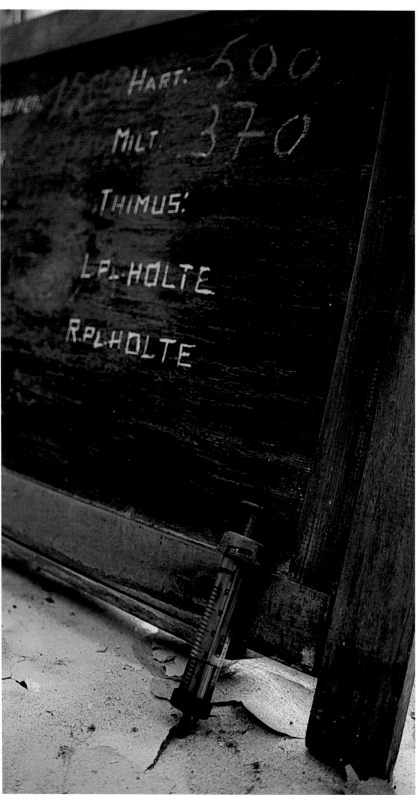

Forensic Institute, Antwerp, Belgium

Saint Vincent's Church

the Netherlands

Keep your faith.

Time passes for the living and for all things.

A false prelude to more profound celebrations.

Vacuity?

If desertion was only illusory?

Favourable to the contemplation of lost souls,
Still not ethereal enough to raise themselves up.
Followers of silent liturgies.

Noise being the seat of vain unrest.
Opening up the spirits with a divine transcendence, this church represents the most perfect incarnation of the Communion.

Sole offering to the elements, it is no longer shaped by anything but wind, rain,

and time.

Humanity will come no more to disturb its atmosphere.

Saint Vincent's Church

Offered to others, it will no longer be burdened by these indiscreet and haughty presences.

All seems in order though to begin the ritual.

What time is the next service?

What will the sermon be about?

The fortuitous visitor, the stray sheep, would be advised to stay in the background.
Who knows, with a little patience, attentiveness and care, he may perceive the manifestation of a devout presence.

Hushed harmony,
a drop has fallen.
That distant sound, is it someone praying, looking for solace?

No, just a pigeon taking flight.

Or is it ...

Saint Vincent's Church, the Netherlands

Saint Vincent's Church, the Netherlands

Saint Vincent's Church, the Netherlands

West Park Mental Hospital

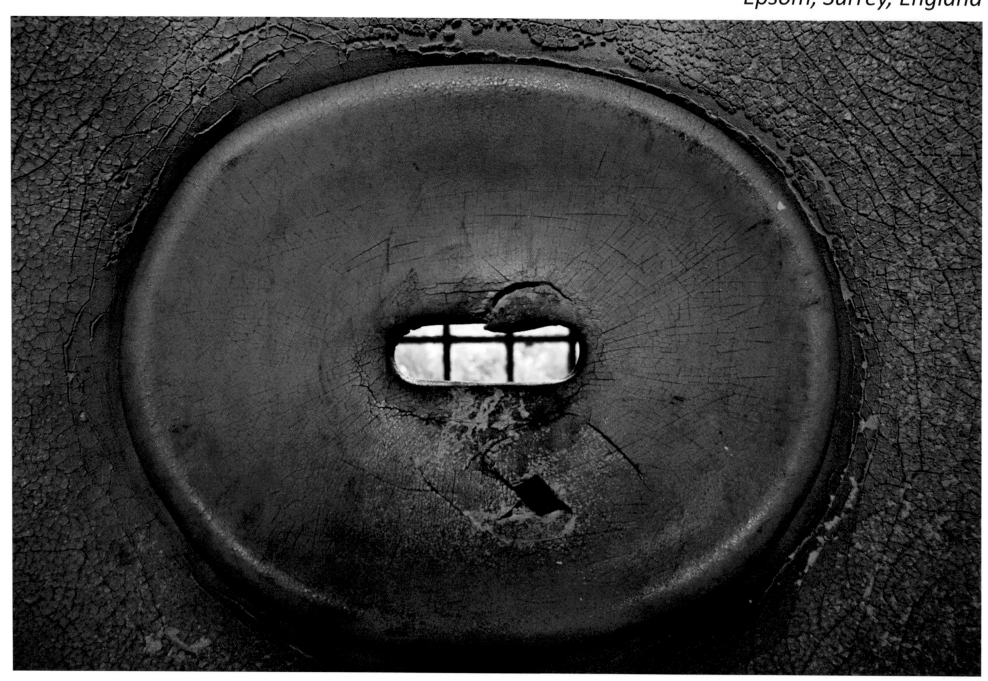

At the end of the 19th century, the London area was served by as many as eleven psychiatric hospitals capable of housing 2,000 patients.

While their Victorian architecture was typical of the time, their organisation evolved with the coming of the 20th century.

West Park was built between 1912 and 1914 in the "Colony" design. The single-sex services were grouped by pathology in wings forming an arrowhead enclosing a wide central corridor.
However, they were all linked by communicating passages. The administrative offices were set in the centre of this vast maze.

The complex was a veritable self-contained village: kitchens, laundries, heating system, water tower, and more. For a number of years, visitors could even take a tram to get around the site.

Treatment was adapted to the most diverse complaints: epilepsy, schizophrenia, anxiety attacks or sudden bouts of delirium.

Each had its own remedy, following the fashion of the time.

West Park Mental Hospital

The policy of Margaret Thatcher known as "Care in the Community" marked a turning point in the British health service. In particular, it sparked off the closure of psychiatric hospitals throughout the country.

Many inmates were thus requested to make other arrangements for their care.

West Park emptied little by little.

It closed its doors for good in the mid 1990s.

The site nevertheless continued to receive occasional visits from former patients, squatters or looters.

The culprit will never be known, but it was probably one of these voyeurs who in 2002 caused the fire that damaged the hospital theatre.

The years rolled by; West Park self-destructed.

Yet this rhythm did not satisfy the authorities, which decided to take matters in hand: the bulldozers will finally snuff out the life of the asylum.

West Park Mental Hospital, Epsom, Surrey, England

West Park Mental Hospital, Epsom, Surrey, England

West Park Mental Hospital, Epsom, Surrey, England

Cheratte Coal Mine

Cheratte, Liège province, Belgium

Another little trip round?

The lift asks only to be filled up again.
For the tunnels, there's plenty of choice.

The winding tower still rises above the pit, dominating Cheratte from its heights.

Boots, mask, pick.

The kit, all complete, seems to wait for us in the changing room.
Trucks swapped for lamps and off it could go again.

In the cage, watching the sky shrink to a single point of light, far above the lighted helmets.
All the "good for the bottom" would be ready to go.

And you could still find some who were.
Seams of good luck.

Yet that's what was missing for the miners of 1970, who saw their colliery close after a century of descents to dig, pick, cut, extract. A few years earlier, there were 1,500 working above ground or in the depths of the mine.

Cheratte Coal Mine, Cheratte, Liège province, Belgium

Cheratte Coal Mine

All concentrating on the precious ore.

Just one generation later, their history has melted away.

The concrete and brick of the neo-medieval buildings began to point to the lack of repairs.

The rare visitors were often looters.

The metalwork rusted away, the showers lost their tiles.

The heritage, abandoned, disappeared.

Soon, the props will collapse; the winches, the furnaces and the equipment will be engulfed among the crumbling seams.

But all said and done, isn't it normal that the earth should want to take back a little of what was torn from it?

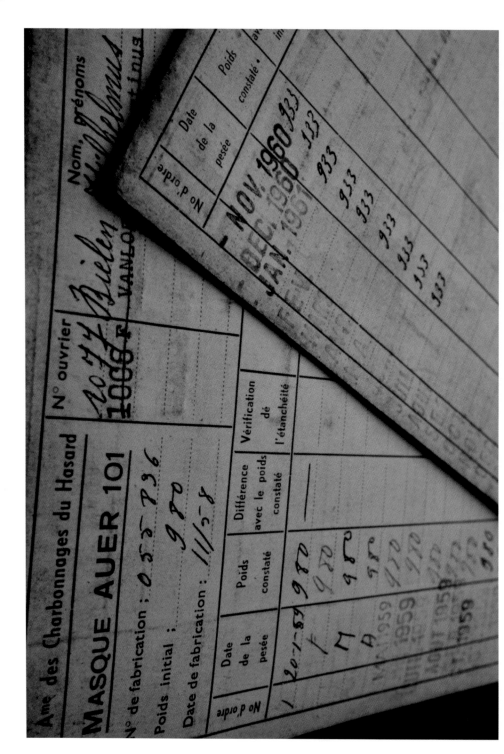

Cheratte Coal Mine, Cheratte, Liège province, Belgium

La salle de pesée des masques à gaz

Cheratte Coal Mine, Cheratte, Liège province, Belgium

Cheratte Coal Mine, Cheratte, Liège province, Belgium

Cheratte Coal Mine, Cheratte, Liège province, Belgium

Cheratte Coal Mine, Cheratte, Liège province, Belgium

Crypt

I remember.

The unhappy past just as the days of glory.

Motto of a nation or of bodies doomed to disappear?

"We have noted that this concession is in an abandoned state. If after a year and a day the maintenance has not been done, we will exhume the coffin and reuse the gravesite. Signed by the guardian, 01/10/1953."

When friends and family have remained in the background.

When even the employees have forgotten that in some corner or another of a crypt lay a neglected corpse below a few old-fashioned funerary ornaments, the peremptory nature of certain administrative procedures may seem pathetic.

Don't they?

Crypt, Quebec

Crypt, Quebec

Crypt, Quebec

Vilvoorde Workhouse

Reform.

It was imposed on Vilvoorde in 1779 under the rule of the Austrian Netherlands.

The construction is as geometric as it is aesthetically displeasing: a large rectangular building divided into several sections.

As many as 12,000 tramps, drunks, and prostitutes, all those that the society of the time considered a nuisance, were crammed in on four floors.

The inside of the prison was primitive, the treatment of the inmates likewise.

The vaulted cells had narrow slits as the only source of light.

A perpetual gloom reigned along the corridors that led to the many workshops.

Subsequently, women, men and children would be separated.
Relatively little comfort …

All were condemned to a long stay.

Vilvoorde Workhouse, Vilvoorde, Brussels, Belgium

Re-education was by means of work; forced labour was the norm.

The inmates turned hemp, wool, and cotton into artisanal goods for sale.

In the 19th century, the building briefly served as a military hospital before reverting to its original use.

In 1914, the army used it first as a barracks then as a detention centre.

The occupying Germans did the same during the Second World War.

Property of the military authorities until 1977, the structure was only used for storage before being abandoned.

The town took it over in 1981, but it was not until 2006 that the cells were listed as a historic monument.

Restoration can begin.

Soon, tourists will shudder while reading the graffiti reflecting the daily grind of the convicts of Reform.

Vilvoorde Workhouse, Vilvoorde, Brussels, Belgium

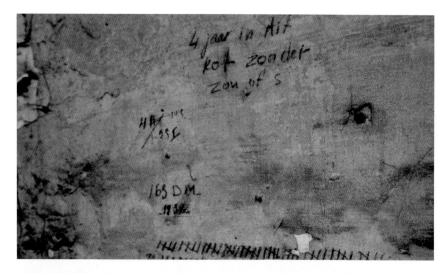

Germaine et Jean rompirent leurs amours le 4/9/1925

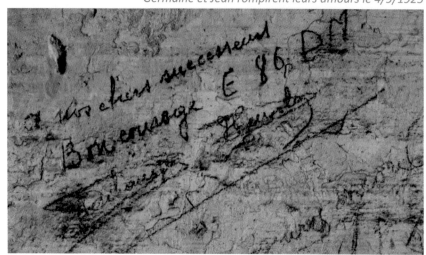

Vilvoorde Workhouse, Vilvoorde, Brussels, Belgium

Twelve Monkeys Power Plant

Baltimore, Maryland.
Westport.

Demolished.
Cleared, levelled.
Deserted.
As if a virus had spread there.
Had contaminated the immense premises of the power plant to make them disappear.

Of this steel and concrete giant, nothing remains.
Nothing other than the railway network that criss-crossed the site so that the silos could be loaded with coal.
It seems there were turbines bigger than cars.
Alternators, thundering steam.

At its construction, in 1906, its colossal size made this power plant the largest ever built.
All that, gone forever.

You might suspect corrosion as the problem, but no.
Rust could not achieve such a work of destruction so quickly – and so completely.
Surgical.

Proof, we've got.

Twelve Monkeys Power Plant, Baltimore, Maryland, United States

Twelve Monkeys Power Plant

When Terry Gilliam used this abandoned site in 1995 as the location for his film, the walls were still standing.

The damage came later.

Was man the cause?
The agent behind its extinction?

The fact is that by 2008, this metal monster was no more.

One day in this very place a hotel or theme park is bound to be built, fronting the waters of Baltimore Bay.

Will walkers and passers-by recall that here stood a power plant, the pride of Baltimore Gas and Electricity?

There's not much chance of that.

Unless we could go back in time to throw light on what really happened ...

Twelve Monkeys Power Plant, Baltimore, Maryland, United States

Twelve Monkeys Power Plant, Baltimore, Maryland, United States

Twelve Monkeys Power Plant, Baltimore, Maryland, United States

Twelve Monkeys Power Plant, Baltimore, Maryland, United States

Twelve Monkeys Power Plant, Baltimore, Maryland, United States

Château de Noisy

The crossing of the ways.
From yesterday to tomorrow.
Noisy will have welcomed noble individuals as well as the homeless.

What would the aristocrat have thought? He who, after his expulsion from the neighbouring château by the sans-culottes, consoled himself by building this immense neo-Gothic edifice?

Château Miranda would suffer the vagaries of the times it lived through.
Beginning with its construction. Despite a century of work, it was never completed as planned.

But no matter — its majesty, its lofty clock tower, its 550 windows, and richly decorated rooms, all in parquet and marble, demand respect.

The family of Count Liedekerke de Beaufort were not ashamed to stay there during their summer vacations.

This residence draws attention.
The best as well as the worst.
So, during the war, it was used as a residence by the occupying Germans.
Conflicts do not last forever.
They fade just like privileges and refinements soften the traces of old habits.

A decade after the liberation, the château was used as a holiday camp by a hundred children of Belgian National Railway Company workers.

Château de Noisy, Celles, Namur province, Belgium

Château de Noisy

The ancient fountain served as a pool for novice swimmers.
The park resounded with the shouts of budding footballers.

But the building found it hard to adapt to its turbulent occupants.
Twenty years caring for children.
Is that enough?

The contract binding the property to the BNRC was not renewed, the count reclaimed his property and the property its calm.
For a while.
For the days when you could keep such a building to yourself have well and truly gone.

Monsieur de Beaufort was once again obliged to rent out his castle.
Seminars, special interest classes, film location ...
Noisy became a burden, a worry.

In 1990, lacking takers and financial help, the count could no longer guarantee the maintenance of his property.
He cleared out.
This time it would be taken over by squatters, vandals and thieves.
Fires, looting, in just a few years château Miranda turned into a ruin, a shell emptied of its contents.

And you can bet that the clock, now stopped, will never start up again.

Château de Noisy, Celles, Namur province, Belgium

Château de Noisy, Celles, Namur province, Belgium

Château de Noisy, Celles, Namur province, Belgium

Château de Noisy, Celles, Namur province, Belgium

Château de Noisy, Celles, Namur province, Belgium

Château de Noisy, Celles, Namur province, Belgium

Krampnitz Barracks

Fancy a bit of training?
Krampnitz is there to help you get into shape.
There's no discrimination here: the soldiers of the 3rd Reich built it, and the Soviet army made use of it until 1992.

Always in a sporting spirit, any activity that keeps you fit can be practised there: handball, basketball, shooting.

Into the bargain, our latest reporter indulged himself in a race, thanks to our mischievous uniformed trainers who spontaneously suggested a game of hide and seek.

The surroundings were considered in the same spirit.
So you will surely be amazed at the paintings brightening up the walls.

Note that they were done by the best official German artists of the 1940s.
As for the Russians who took over, whose style of architecture is easily recognisable, they too were quite naturally inclined to decorate their buildings with frescoes, which add some feeling to their handiwork.

Do you feel lazy, lethargic or tired?

Krampnitz will cure your idleness.

Krampnitz Barracks, Krampnitz, Potsdam, Germany

Krampnitz Barracks, Krampnitz, Potsdam, Germany

Krampnitz Barracks, Krampnitz, Potsdam, Germany

Krampnitz Barracks, Krampnitz, Potsdam, Germany

Tours & Taxis

Brussels, Belgium

When the Torre de Tassi family, from noble Italian stock, settled in Austria, they became Thurn und Taxis.
The history of the dynasty began to be written.

As early as the 13th century they were involved in the courier business.
As this service expanded, an authentic international postal service was born.
Trade created relationships. The family also exported itself throughout Europe.

François de Taxi was one of the promoters of these messenger services.
He lived in Brussels, near the port and the junction of the Willebroek and Charleroi canals.

This strategic location facilitated the rapid growth of his service and thus of the site.

In the 17th century, the family moved its headquarters to Austria.
No matter. In Belgium, the business was well established.

The 19th century saw the end of the mail service monopoly.
Thurn und Taxis decided to sell the site.

The city bought it and sold the franchise to Tours & Taxis.

A good bargain?

It was just the beginning.

Tours & Taxis, Brussels, Belgium

Warehouses were built and hangars sprang up while the railway was extended to link land and sea.

To regulate the traffic, a customs post was set up in a respectable brick and stone building given pride of place at the heart of the site.

Thurn und Taxis was by then spread over 37 hectares and, at the beginning of the 20th century, had become one of the largest transport companies in the country.

Free trade in Europe perhaps had something to do with it.

But the formerly essential work of the customs post became obsolete with the lifting of trade barriers.

It was condemned to close its great doors.

Victims of changes in the transport system, one after another the surrounding buildings were obliged to do likewise.

Ironically enough, the mail service was the last to cease trading.

It finally moved out in 1987.

Tours & Taxis was disused for the next ten years.

In 2007, it built a new life on the ruins of the former one: the old buildings, filled with souvenirs, were restored as a site of multicultural development.

Another trade-in.

Tours & Taxis, Brussels, Belgium

Tours & Taxis, Brussels, Belgium

Varia Cinema-Theatre

Silence!
The story begins ...
At the corner of a little street.

No more space is needed for this building to play a full part on the Charleroi scene.

To catch the eye, a concrete façade fitted with a monumental balcony.

Welcome to the Varia Cinema-Theatre.

Single-handedly promising grand shows.

However, on approaching, you sense that something is amiss.

The show's over?

Now it's on the door and not on the stage that the boards take their stance.

Since 1910, this building has however had its chance.
In seventy years, at least three generations have paraded before its pediment.

Attracted more by operettas or popular films (on Sundays, two seats for the price of one!) than by its Art Nouveau façade, the population of Charleroi, in complete turmoil at the time, gladly met up there.

Varia Cinema-Theatre, Jumet, Hainaut province, Belgium

Varia Cinema-Theatre

One room to meet in, one interval to talk about it.

The darkness of a film to make sure the chemistry is right.

Without knowing it, these spectators, miners or steelworkers, were often forging what were to become memories.

For in 1986 the death knell sounded for the theatricals.

Screens and curtains were hung up for good.

The multicoloured paintings were covered, the lyrical moulding and baroque gilding masked.

On to the subculture.

Decadence?

The theatre was briefly transformed into a dance floor.

The listing of its façade wasn't enough to make a success of the disco.

The doors were closed for good.

Twilight enveloped the set.

And though the reinforced concrete could resist the flames, it could do nothing against time.

The stage was scattered with plaster dust.
Saltpetre covered the theatre.
Had we come to the end of the story?

The red curtain, still stiffly hanging there, may well lose patience.

Even if these last years have seen several conversion projects put forward, things have not been well in the region for some time …

In the early 2000s, the Institut du Patrimoine Wallon proposed setting up a Centre of Visual Arts there, but work was stopped for lack of funds.

Let's hope that isn't the last tale to be told at the Varia.

Varia Cinema-Theatre, Jumet, Hainaut province, Belgium

Varia Cinema-Theatre, Jumet, Hainaut province, Belgium

Varia Cinema-Theatre, Jumet, Hainaut province, Belgium

Varia Cinema-Theatre, Jumet, Hainaut province, Belgium

Varia Cinema-Theatre, Jumet, Hainaut province, Belgium

Synchronisation Studio

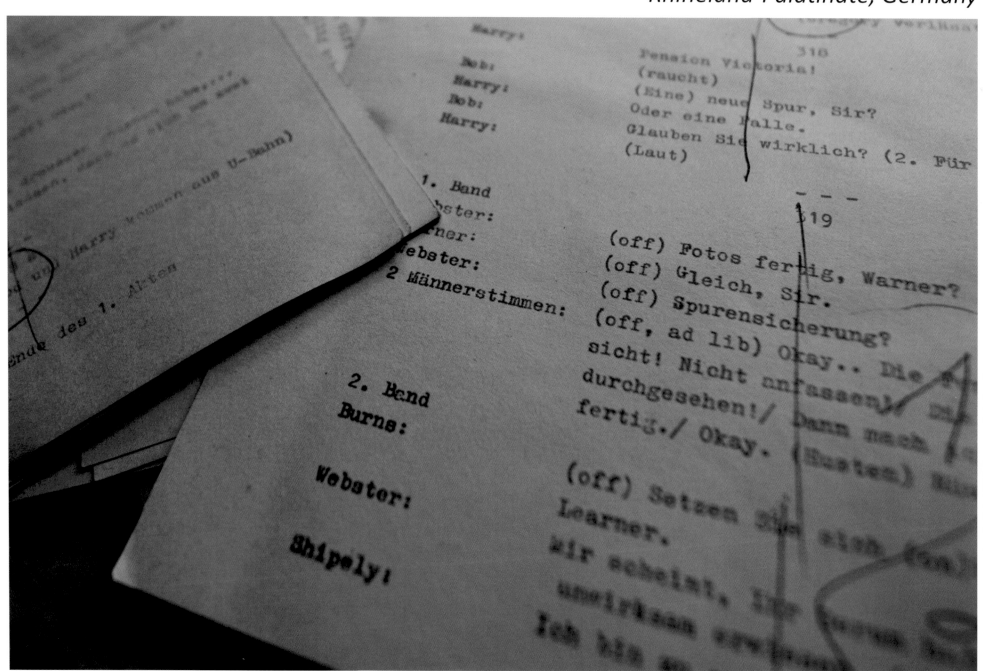

Immersion in the Calmuth valley.

A production by the International Film Union, supported by UGC.

The story begins in 1947.
It is set in the former property of Deutsches Jungvolk, future Hitler Youth, and is an account of the fate of the best-known West German cinematic synchronisation company.

Originally, the ambitious project foresaw a production department, projection and audience auditoriums, dubbing and mixing booth and facilities to cater for the actors during their stay.

For financial reasons, all this was scaled down.

Nevertheless, over 800 films were dubbed into a number of languages.
On the credits, Romy Schneider, Harald Juhnke, René Deltgen …

Fast forward to the sixties:
There was plenty of work for the International Film Union.
The copying of inflammable cellulose film onto a fireproof medium was added to its workload.

600,000 films were duplicated in this way each year.

Synchronisation Studio

In 1967, the spontaneous combustion of cellulose nitrate caused an explosion that destroyed a large part of the reels stored at Calmuth.

The damage was incalculable.

As its location in the heart of the forest guaranteed tranquility, and sound recordings could be made there to best effect, orders continued to flow in before dropping off little by little.

Work became scarce.
In 1996, copying was stopped.

The last scene shows the equipment and locations beginning to disintegrate.

Yet the outcome isn't a tragedy: bought out by a wealthy property-owner, the premises will be converted into a hunting lodge.

The beginning of another story.

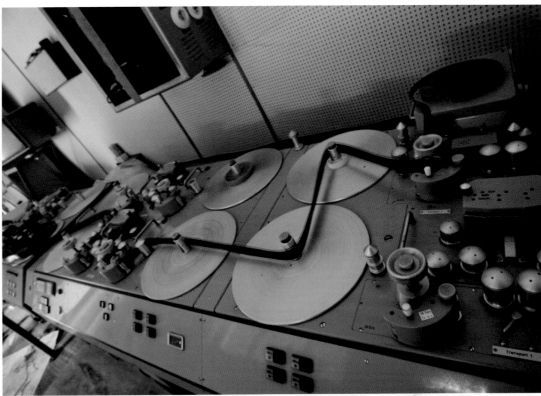

Synchronisation Studio, Rhineland-Palatinate, Germany

Synchronisation Studio, Rhineland-Palatinate, Germany

Synchronisation Studio, Rhineland-Palatinate, Germany

Synchronisation Studio, Rhineland-Palatinate, Germany

Mesen Castle

I will maintain.
The motto of the site.
The memory of the ancestors.
Four centuries of construction in the grip of decay.
Scant opposition to lordly elegance.
What would the Bette family think?

The marquis himself had solicited the skill of the best Italian master architects to decorate Mesen Castle and its many outbuildings scattered around the 7 hectare park. A bygone era?

The 19th century advocated utilitarianism.
The imposing size of the cellar windows suggested a good use for the building.
From 1791, the building served as a centre for local production.
Alcohol, tobacco, refined sugar …
In 1897, the Order of Saint Augustine bought the property and turned over a new page in its history: the end of production.

It was the minds of local young girls that would be moulded.
The place was asking for it.

They had to put their stamp on it to make it their own.
The canonesses decided to build an edifice befitting its grandeur.

In 1905, the respectable neo-Gothic chapel was erected.
The site was henceforth spiritual.

Mesen Castle, Lede, East Flanders province, Belgium

Mesen Castle

After 1918, the Institut Royal de Messine made its home there. Founded by Madame de Maintenon, it advocated an elitist and strict secular education for young ladies of good family.
The proprieties of etiquette.
Classes were held only in French.
Curtseys, formalities.

In 1970, the boarding school whose style had become outmoded closed its doors. It fell into the hands of the Ministry of Defence.
Had the habitation, used to a noble society, failed in its final transformation?
The new owner, unable to satisfy its costly demands, let the castle waste away. It was officially made a protected site in 1974, but a bureaucratic blunder meant that it lost that status a year later.

Its decline became inevitable.
Brambles took over the orangery.
The interior woodwork rotted.

The castle slowly slid towards its present state.
Ruined.
Yet it was still standing when its demolition was announced in 2007.
The opulence is gone.

It only has to await with dignity its last visitors:
The bulldozers.

Mesen Castle, Lede, East Flanders province, Belgium

Mesen Castle, Lede, East Flanders province, Belgium

Mesen Castle, Lede, East Flanders province, Belgium

Mesen Castle, Lede, East Flanders province, Belgium

1936 Olympic Village

Wustermark, Brandenburg, Germany

In 1931, Berlin won
The right to offer the athletes of the entire world an
Olympic site
For the Games of 1936.

The town threw itself into the construction of pharaonic
structures. They would allow 4,000 selected athletes to
compete, and rest, in the best possible conditions.
Five years to think big.

Meanwhile, the country had sold its soul to National
Socialism.
The new regime saw in these games the opportunity to
demonstrate its power to the world.
To succeed with such a project, it mobilised all available
resources even though the country was in crisis.
So, a 120,000-seat stadium was erected.

In their accommodation on the Wustermark site, west of
Berlin, the competitors were well catered for.
The term Olympic Village was not taken in vain because
the 145 buildings constructed for the occasion formed
an authentic urban space organised around sport and
relaxation. This mushrooming town was home to a
specialised hospital, shops, cinema, theatre, library
and a plethora of refreshment points. Lodgings were in
individual rooms, each personalised and fitted with the
most modern amenities.

The sporting facilities were also planned so as to allow
the athletes to train until the last minute.

1936 Olympic Village, Wustermark, Brandenburg, Germany

The Games had 129 competitions, for which there were many entries.
Demand was satisfied thanks to the many practice halls built within the village itself.
A pool allowed even the swimmers to train and the others to relax before a sauna session!

The construction and the functioning of this architectural complex, in the shape of a horseshoe, were under the responsibility of Wolfgang Fürstner.
It could have been a dream come true but we know the rest of the story.
Wolfgang Fürstner, who was of Jewish stock, was dismissed from his post during the Games. He committed suicide two days after they closed.

Three months later, the village was converted into a military school.

After the war, it retained its martial air, now in the service of the Soviet forces, and then was gradually abandoned with the breakup of the Eastern bloc.

Today, only a few sections have been restored.

The rest has returned to the mists of its ambiguous past.

1936 Olympic Village, Wustermark, Brandenburg, Germany

1936 Olympic Village, Wustermark, Brandenburg, Germany

1936 Olympic Village, Wustermark, Brandenburg, Germany

1936 Olympic Village, Wustermark, Brandenburg, Germany

1936 Olympic Village, Wustermark, Brandenburg, Germany

Malines Cloister

Brothers, Malines monastery is truly ours:
By stripping it of its original splendour, its dereliction has come to symbolise our mendicant order.

Since the 18th century and our forced departure, many have wished to take it over.

Without success.

Other religious orders have settled here; the French military have used it as a hospital. They could not stay here.

In 1977, they decamped.

The dust has progressively fallen on it, protecting it with a layer of white, like a Dominican tunic.

Since then, nobody has been able to return to achieve their ambitions.

Therefore we should praise this decline; it reflects a rallying call to the word of Saint Dominic.

Malines Cloister, Malines, Antwerp province, Belgium

Malines Cloister, Malines, Antwerp province, Belgium

Malines Cloister, Malines, Antwerp province, Belgium

Gary, Indiana

The moving destiny of a hundred-year-old town.
When the American steel company set up its headquarters in this corner of Indiana, it initiated the rise of a new city that naturally took the name of Gary, the surname of its president.

The steelworks prospered, and the town did, too.

Recruitment was easy; the highway of dunes that linked Chicago to Detroit pulled in travellers.

People flocked there.
The mixed-race city would grow to a population of 200,000.

Among them were Joseph and Katherine Jackson.
He was a worker and she was a housewife, raising their nine children as well as they could.
The seventh, the little Michael Joseph, sometimes sang along with his brothers and sisters.
Throughout his career, the great Michael Jackson would remember his hometown.

A flourishing industry, well-developed communications, celebrities …
Who would have believed that the metropolis was a future desert?

In the 1960s, the local steel industry began to suffer from competition.
The United States Steel Corporation relocated, leaving the local workforce high and dry.

Gary, Indiana

The white population, often better off, went away to try their luck elsewhere. The white flight.
Those who stayed had to face an economy that was running down.
The black market thrived. Criminality came to town.
Gary took the prize for the most dangerous town in the United States.
Education declined.

On the heels of the industrial buildings, the cultural centres would also close, victims of the drop in visitors.
Whole districts were emptied of their residents.
The faithful few remaining, disillusioned, no longer believed in redemption.
They abandoned their church, which finally collapsed for lack of regular maintenance.

The town was dying.
Would it bury itself in the sand on which it stood?
In the early 2000s, people held on to hope.
The airport was restored, and investment encouraged, while the municipality proclaimed a crimewatch policy.

Various schemes were started in an attempt to wipe out the past and turn towards a hopefully brighter future.

Yet Gary, a semi-ghost town, will have a lot of trouble ridding itself of the spectres that continue to haunt it.

Gary, Indiana, State of Indiana, United States

L'entrée de l'opéra de Gary

Gary, Indiana, State of Indiana, United States

Saint-Martin Metro Station

Paris, France

The rush hour's over!
At least, you'd think so.
Judging by the deserted platforms.

A train passes.

But time doesn't.

At the junction of one of the oldest lines in the capital,
there should be crowds around.

But all is at a standstill.

The advertising hoardings, between tiles and faded paper,
bear witness to bygone days.
A time when over thirty thousand passengers an hour
passed through.

A train passes.

Sometimes the roles are reversed.
Some stops were indeed moved elsewhere, merged or
recycled for various uses.

Other stations were never opened or, out-of-the-way,
never saw a single carriage draw up at their platforms.
This one was closed during the war.

Saint-Martin Metro Station, Paris, France

Reopened shortly afterwards, and although heavily used, it was sentenced to become a spectator of the suburban RATP service due to its close proximity to the following stops.

To liven things up, there is always the ephemeral visit of a graffiti artist or the occasional trainspotter.
In winter, the homeless chat as they warm themselves in the centre opened up for them near the former ticket offices.

Are the daily commuters from Île-de-France still interested in this station?
Surely no more than a passing train ...

Saint-Martin Metro Station, Paris, France

Saint-Martin Metro Station, Paris, France

Uhart-Mixe Manor

For sale,
In the heart of a charming Basque village.
Ancient building (1518) of three storeys.

Many outbuildings (tower, dovecote listed as a historic monument).

Structure regularly modernised (1699: extra wing; 1833: extra height)

Interior decoration that may be of interest to lovers of rock paintings.

Building suitable for professional use (children's holiday camp, legal practice, etc.) or personal use.

Private garden (two hectares) including a site offering good irrigation (located on a floodplain).

Some work required (roof, electricity, insulation, land clearance ... estimated at 2 million euros)

Don't hesitate to view the photos taken by our agent to get a better idea of this most attractive offer.

The bargain of the century.

Take note!

Uhart-Mixe Manor, Uhart-Mixe, Pyrénées-Atlantiques, France

Uhart-Mixe Manor, Uhart-Mixe, Pyrénées-Atlantiques, France

Uhart-Mixe Manor, Uhart-Mixe, Pyrénées-Atlantiques, France

Uhart-Mixe Manor, Uhart-Mixe, Pyrénées-Atlantiques, France

Hôtel Monjouste

If you are passing by Bigorre,
Looking for a breath of fresh air.
Stop awhile at Hôtel Monjouste.

A little detour to remind you what it was like to be a child,
Before.

Lovely holidays, between amusement
And contemplation.

The ideal spot to go and discover nature.
You missed the izard as it leaped away?

You can always take your time watching its cousin,
Stuffed.

Here, they know how to comfort discontented youth.

Quieted down?

Beginnings of a sweet rest to come?

If we no longer hear young laughter resound.

It's because, here, the youthful years have long ago faded …

Hôtel Monjouste, Betharram, Hautes-Pyrénées, France

Hôtel Monjouste, Betharram, Hautes-Pyrénées, France

Rochendaal Castle

A family story.
Ulens.

Two cousins.

At first distant, then growing closer.

Until wedding bells rang out.

The young newly-weds could then think of settling down.

Starting a family.

That is how Rochendaal Castle came to be built.

The story of a town.
Saint Truiden.

Monsieur Ulens became mayor. A local dignitary, a lawyer to boot, he owed it to himself to possess a residence worthy of his position.
The house was magnificently decorated and dressed in ornaments of the late 19th century.

To welcome the Ulens children and their descendants could have been the home's destiny. The story would have peacefully perpetuated itself.

Instead, it came up against the homeland and came of age.

Rochendaal Castle

Located in a military zone during the Second World War, the residence became the headquarters of the Belgian and then the German forces.

As a strategic base, it was equipped with three landing strips but kept its role as officers' accommodation.

The fighting over, the air force of the kingdom of Belgium was reinstated within its walls and it was the turn of the pilots and cadets to settle there.

Functional and strategically located, the castle would nevertheless be deserted in 1996 because of the high cost of maintenance.

Today, the runways are still sometimes used as a playground for fans of motor sports while the rest disappears little by little under the quiet onslaught of the vegetation.

End of story?

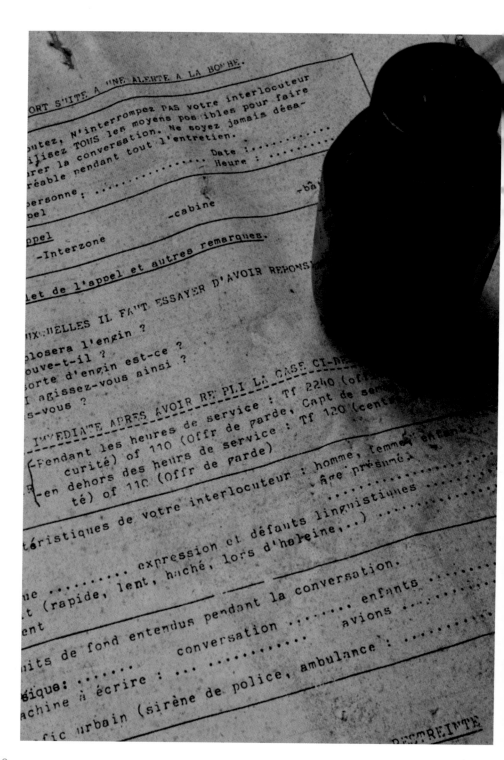

Rochendaal Castle, Saint-Trond, Limbourg province, Belgium

Rochendaal Castle, Saint-Trond, Limbourg province, Belgium

Rochendaal Castle, Saint-Trond, Limbourg province, Belgium

Portopalo Castle

I dreamed of a palace.

Perched on top of a cliff, it overlooked the sea from its lofty heights.
Its interior played cleverly with light.
The sun warmed its walls of ochre stone. Yet the greenery of the patio allowed the morning freshness to linger a little longer.

Here and there in the vast salon, wide staircases unwound.
They led to luminous terraces overlooking the ocean.
The windows were dressed with cleverly wrought iron.
All seemed calm, peaceful.

Suddenly, time speeded up.
A morning, then an evening.
Another day.
Then, darkness.

When the sun rose once more, all had aged.
The plants had taken over the garden.
The panes of the orangery had broken.
All seemed abandoned, lifeless.

I awoke and reality flooded back:
I was in the abandoned castle of Portopalo di Capo Passero.

Portopalo Castle, Portopalo di Capo Passero, Syracuse province, Sicily

Portopalo Castle, Portopalo di Capo Passero, Syracuse province, Sicily

Acknowledgements

The authors would particularly like to thank their family and friends for their constant encouragement throughout the writing of this book.
They would also like to thank Martine Azoulai for the precision of her criticisms, Alain Labarrère-Brosou for his linguistic skills and availability and, of course, Thomas Jonglez for having believed in this project.

Sylvain would like to thank Ann-Charlotte for her presence and constant support, Henk van Rensbergen, Yves Marchand and Tom Kirsch, who are inexhaustible sources of inspiration, and everyone who contributed to this project in any way, large or small: Angelo Stiliaras, Nicolas Elias, Aurélie Selle of the RATP, as well as all his guides and exploring companions: Elle Dunn, Vincent Duseigne, Nick and Hilary Santangelo, Paul and Gonnie Tieman, Seth Thomas...

David would like to thank Céline for her unwavering psychological and culinary support, the community of free developers for their tools and, of course, Sylvain for having let him take part in this beautiful project.

Photos:
All photos were taken by Sylvain Margaine. The photos of the Saint-Martin metro station were taken under the supervision of and published with the kind authorization of the RATP.

Layout: Stéphanie Benoit
Translation: Caroline Lawrence
Editing-correction: Kimberley Bess